向陽

EX·LIBRIS

Grass Roots

SELECTED POEMS

向陽

Xiang Yang

TRANSLATED BY

John Balcom

ZEPHYR PRESS

BROOKLINE, MA

Cover and interior woodcuts by Xiang Yang
Book design by *type*slowly

Zephyr Press, a non-profit arts and education 501(c)(3) organization,
publishes literary titles that foster a deeper understanding of cultures
and languages. Zephyr Press books are distributed to the trade in the U.S.
and Canada by Consortium Book Sales and Distribution [www.cbsd.com]
and by Small Press Distribution [www.spdbooks.org].

Zephyr Press acknowledges with gratitude the financial support of the
Massachusetts Cultural Council and the National Museum of Taiwan
Literature, which assisted in the translation and publication of this book.

massculturalcouncil.org

Cataloguing-in publication data is available from the Library of Congress.

ISBN 978-1-938890-07-9

ZEPHYR PRESS
50 Kenwood Street
Brookline, MA 02446

www.zephyrpress.org

Contents

Ten-line Poems

Dialect Poems

A Miscellany

The Four Seasons

Introduction

Xiang Yang (Hsiang Yang, 向陽) is the penname of Lin Qiyang. He was born in Nantou, central Taiwan on May 7, 1955, and grew up in a village where his family ran a small shop. One of the more significant voices to emerge in post-retrocession Taiwan, his significance as a poet is founded on a number of factors. In his work, he has successfully blended the traditional and the modern, practiced a new formalism, penned narrative poetry and a major poetic sequence, and was an early proponent of dialect poetry in Taiwan. Among his collections of poetry are: *Looking Up at the Gingko Tree* (1977), *Seeds* (1980), *Ten-line Poems* (1984), *Time* (1985), *Songs of the Soil* (1985), *The Four Seasons* (1986), *My Cares* (1987), *Selected Poems 1974–1996* (1999), *Taiwanese Poems* (2002), *Chaos* (2005). He is also an essayist of note and a woodblock print artist. For many years he worked as an editor at a newspaper and now teaches.

Early in life, he developed an interest in Tang poetry, which remained a passion for many years. However, the formative literary experience occurred while he was in junior high school when he plunged into the *Li Sao*, a long narrative poem about a scorned minister of state, attributed to China's first poet Chu Yuan. The poem contains lush descriptions of the flora and fauna of the southern mainland.

"It was through a misunderstanding on my part that I ever picked up the *Li Sao*," Xiang Yang says. "Being somewhat romantically inclined, I thought it was a long love poem. You can imagine my surprise when I opened the book. It's hardly a book for a thirteen-year-old boy. But working through the poem awakened in me the desire to write poetry. My later experiments in poetic form and the strong sense of place in my work owe much to reading the *Li Sao*."

Rural Taiwan and its landscape are present in many of Xiang Yang's poems. Landscape and rural poems have a long history in China, generally depicting the court or city as decadent places exercising a corrupting influence. In many contemporary poems from Taiwan, the sense of alienation one associates with modern life is viewed as a largely urban phenomenon, whereas all healthy values reside in the countryside. But this dichotomy, which is also seen as a shortcoming of such contemporary poetry, is itself a significant part of the local literary tradition of Nativism, which emerged during the Japanese occupation (1895–1945) as writers and artists sought to articulate a sense of Taiwan identity.

The young poet first encountered modern vernacular poetry in the fifth grade, when he read the works of Xu Zhimo and Zhu Ziqing and began to imitate them. But it was not until high school that he first encountered the high modernist poetry then being written in Taiwan—he bought copies of Yu Guangzhong's *Associations of the Lotus*, Ya Xian's *Abyss*, Lo Fu's *River Without Banks* and collections of essays on poetry and poetics by Qin Zihao and Lo Men. Reading the best of contemporary poetry alongside the masterpieces of the classical canon, he wondered if vernacular poetry could ever attain the beauty and perfection of poems by Tao Qian, Xie Lingyun, Li Po, and Du Fu. It seemed an impossible task, and one that has constantly preoccupied him.

While studying Japanese language and literature at the Chinese Culture University in Taipei, Xiang Yang began to consider his past work, which seemed to lack direction and depth, and seriously contemplate the road he was going to take as a poet. His own views and experiences were at odds with many aspects of current modernist poetics. Like many young poets of the day, he was becoming disillusioned with high modernist writing; the elitist movement and its individualistic and frequently nihilistic verse were turning into an empty formalism. Furthermore, much modernist writing was starting to be perceived as a puerile imitation of Western writing. Younger poets began looking closely at the Chinese literary tradition, both classical and modern.

The so-called "third generation poets," such as Xiang Yang, Du Ye, and Lo Qing, wanted to see a resurgence of Chinese national and local culture after years of foreign domination. In Taiwan, this revival was complex and multifaceted: the trend toward Westernization in the cultural sphere was subverted by a resurgence of interest in traditional Chinese culture, and political domination by the Kuomintang from the Mainland was opposed by promotion of Taiwanese language and culture. Xiang Yang himself eventually decided to explore two avenues: to write poetry in his native southern Min dialect and to experiment with formalist verse. "I asked myself what made classical poems so enduring," he says. "It seemed to me that the strict compositional rules and forms of classical poetry contributed greatly to poetic quality." He began experimenting with forms and rhyme, finally settling on a ten-line poem broken into two quintets as the form most suited to his temperament. It can be said that form made a poet out of him: formal limitations helped to channel and structure the poetic impulse.

Xiang Yang wrote his first ten-line poem, "Listening to the Rain," in 1974. Most of his ten-line poems were written over the next decade. While the form remained the same, theme and content changed and developed through three roughly chronological phases. The first (1974–1976) is represented by the twenty or so poems in his first book *Looking Up at the Gingko Tree*, and are largely concerned with personal emotions of love, nostalgia, and homesickness. His poem "Small Station," written in 1976, is a typical example:

> Isn't it like
> That small red flower
> Standing timidly in the gloom
> Under the golden gingko grove of home
> Soaked in the rain last autumn?
>
> Away from home this spring, from the train at dusk
> I see an egret
> Flap its ash-white wings
> Soar among crimson clouds
> And disappear!

In the first quintet, the speaker recalls his home, specifically a small, solitary red flower seen the previous autumn. In the second, the focus shifts to what the speaker is seeing now from a train window the following spring. Between time remembered and time present, the speaker has left home. Now, sitting in a train, he sees an egret take flight. Here, the egret can stand as a manifestation of the speaker's own feelings of aloneness in the vast world.

Structurally, the poem follows the traditional thematic progression of a classical Tang poem, which partitions a poem into four parts—*qi*, *cheng, zhuan, he*, or beginning, development, turn, and conclusion. The poem begins with the image of a small red flower, an image further developed and enriched in the description of the gingko grove. The second quintet initiates a turn —in this case a change in time and place. The poem ends by fusing time present and time past in the image of the soaring egret, itself an imaginative correlative to the flower image.

In his ten-line poems, Xiang Yang frequently resorts to the three traditional compositional techniques that developed out of the early exegesis of the *Book of Songs*, China's first poetry anthology—*xing*, or motif, *bi*, or metaphor, and *fu*, or narrative display. In the poem quoted, the egret image can stand as a metaphor for the speaker's own thoughts and feelings. And much like a traditional nature poem, the speaker's experience is manifested in an inherent antithetical structure in which for a particular scene there must be a subjective consciousness to respond to it. Thus, while Xiang Yang's poems are written in the modern vernacular, they obey many of the rules of classical verse.

In the second phase (1977–1981), Xiang Yang wrote another thirty ten-line poems, most of which were published in his 1980 collection *Seeds*. There are still many landscape poems, but also poems about objects in the classical *yongwu* tradition—poems about objects that describe by analogy abstract feelings or human qualities. The third stage (1982–1984) also shows a shift in thematic concern toward poems of social concern. The language tends to be less polished, more colloquial and matter-of-fact. The twenty-one poems of this stage were included in his third collection of poetry, *Ten-line Poems*, and were written after he graduated from college and began working. Many of the poems written during this stage focus on the adult world and a loss of innocence; the simple joys of childhood and the romantic idealism of youth have given way to adult feelings of unhappiness, conflict, defeat, and compromise.

At the same time Xiang Yang was experimenting with formalist verse, he also struck out in another direction and began writing poems in his native southern Min dialect. For a poet, there are advantages and disadvantages to using dialect: while the southern Min dialect, also commonly referred to as Taiwanese, is spoken by 70 percent of the population of Taiwan, the written form of the language has never been standardized. Thus reading and writing poetry written in the dialect takes some effort. However, Mandarin cannot match the expressive powers of the dialect for a native speaker, and some poets insist that the reality of Taiwan can only be expressed through use of the dialect.

When Xiang Yang began writing dialect poetry, the use of Taiwanese was still a sensitive issue—he was criticized for advocating separatism—but he persisted. "When I was in college in Taipei," he says, "the turmoil in my life and in cultural circles forced me to look at my roots in the countryside. I thought of the people I knew and loved at home, their joys and sorrows, and wanted to write about them. But I wanted to do it in a language they spoke."

Having no formal education in reading and writing Taiwanese, Xiang Yang's first attempts were naturally slow and painful: "I kept the rhythms of opera and puppet theatre in my head when I started writing, and then I found the words to fit the rhythms," he says. "Then I wrote what I had in my mind, character by character, line by line. It was very slow going at first." Rural life, work, and politics are the predominate themes.

During his obligatory military service, Xiang Yang contemplated writing a long historical narrative poem about Taiwan, but it was not until he returned to civilian life that he had time to make this idea a reality. In 1978, he wrote "Wushe," a narrative poem about the 1930 Wushe Incident, when Seediq tribes people in the small mountain village took up arms against the Japanese colonial rulers. The six-part poem subsequently won the *China Times* poetry award. The Incident was immediately seized upon at the time as a symbol of Japan's oppression of Taiwan—Lai He, the father of modern Taiwan literature wrote a poem titled "Lament for the South in 1930." The Incident still had resonance for Xiang Yang as he employed it for critical ends and in the ongoing process of articulating a Taiwan identity as well as demonstrating his ability to write narrative poetry. Many indigenous people, who see themselves as oppressed by the Han Chinese majority, view the appropriation of the Incident to construct a Taiwan identity as ironic at best, as simply yet another instance of cultural imperialism. Most recently the incident was the subject of Wei Te-sheng's 2011 film *Seediq Bale*.

To date, Xiang Yang's magnum opus is without a doubt his poetic sequence *The Four Seasons*, published in 1986. The sequence combines many of the qualities of his previous work: the formalism of his ten-line poems, the use of dialect, the abiding presence of the Taiwan landscape, and a strong social consciousness. The twenty-four poems in the collection, one for each of the twenty-four periods of the traditional Chinese agricultural calendar, provide the reader with a comprehensive picture of Taiwan in the 1980s.

The early poems in the sequence tend to be landscape poems in which man lives in harmony with nature. As the sequence progresses, however, the rural orientation gradually shifts, the urban intrudes ever more, and a somber tone gradually takes hold. The collection spans the seasons and the changes they bring to Taiwan, the socioeconomic development of the island, as well as encompassing the whole spectrum of human moods and emotions.

From start to finish, the collection is an articulation of Taiwan's identity imbued with salient cultural details. In the poem titled "Hoar Frost," for example, the references to popular songs are telling. Take the 1946 song "Mending Broken Nets." In Taiwanese, the word for "nets" is homophonous with the word for "hopes." The song was originally penned to lament a broken love, but later took on political significance. For many years the song was banned on television. "Buy My Dumplings" deals with the difficulties that the people of Taiwan faced just after the Japanese left the island and returned it to Chinese control. Both songs stand as living expressions of the memory of the recent past and, over the years since they were written, both have helped define a sense of a Taiwan identity.

Xiang Yang's poetry stands as elegant testimony to the Taiwan experience. The range and formal variety of his work is truly impressive. However, since the publication of *The Four Seasons*, he has written little, publishing but a single collection titled *Chaos*, in 2005. In the intervening years, he has earned a PhD in journalism and moved from journalism to academia, devoting himself to teaching.

Acknowledgments

I first encountered Xiang Yang's poetry over thirty years ago when I was a young student in Taipei. I still remember the day I found a copy of his first collection of poetry in a bookstore on Chongqing South Road. I enjoyed reading it so much that I immediately set about translating some of his early ten-line poems. In the ensuing years, I followed Xiang Yang's career as a poet with interest and continued to translate his poetry. I wish to thank him for his support and friendship over what has now become decades. Thanks also to *The Taipei Chinese PEN* and *The Taipei Review* in which some of these translations first appeared and to Columbia University Press for permission to reprint a number of translations from *Frontier Taiwan*, to University of Washington Press and Unitas for permission to reprint "Discovering □□" from *Sailing to Formosa*, and to Taoran Press for permission to reprint *The Four Seasons*, which was originally published as a chapbook and is now long out of print. Portions of the preface to this edition appeared originally in an article on Xiang Yang written for the *Taipei Review* and I'm pleased to be able to quote from it. Acknowledgment is also due to the National Museum of Taiwan Literature for financial support of this project. Thanks also to Christopher Mattison of Zephyr Press for his continued editorial work. Lastly, I wish to express my heartfelt gratitude to Yingtsih, my wife, whose help has been inestimable.

Ten-line Poems

聽雨

坐在山的這一邊，遙遙地
聽見那邊谷地，恍恍惚惚
傳來陣陣呼喊，淅淅瀝瀝
驚醒了我，築巢採果的
美夢

於是走向谷地去，翼翼地
發現一株啜泣的野蘭，當我
伸手撫慰，乃又了然那花
是昔日，淅淅瀝瀝呼喊的
聲音

1974

Listening to the Rain

Sitting on this side of the mountain, far away
Faint cries are heard from the valley below
I am awakened from a beautiful dream
Of a simple life
By the sound of rain

Making my way to the valley floor
I discover a weeping orchid, I realize
As I reach out to soothe it, that this flower
Is the sound of rain crying
From days gone by

懷人

那座山岡，自君別後
已孤獨靜默了許久
今晨我去，發現前年
我們踩過幽徑的松子
仍舊紛紛走回松林的枝枒

那條小路，在斜陽下
更崎嶇斑駁了許多
前年此刻，送君遠行
我們臨觴釃酒的亭腳
竟然長滿隨風飄搖的艾草

1976

Thinking of a Friend

That mountain, since we parted
Has stood so long in lonely silence
This morning, I found on that dark path
The pine cones we had trod year before last
Had all returned to the branches

Under the slanting sunlight, that small path
Is rougher and more mottled
This time, year before last, when I saw you off
At the foot of the pavilion where we shared a drink
Thick grows the sagebrush blowing in the wind

小站

彷彿還是去年秋天
被雨打濕了金黃羽翼的
故鄉的銀杏林下，那朵
畏縮地站在一抹陰翳蒼茫中
鮮紅的，小花？

透過今春異地黃昏的車窗
望去：一隻鷺鷥
　　　舞動著灰白的雙翅
　　　在緋麗的晚雲裏，翩翩
飛逸！

1976

Train Station

Isn't it like
That small red flower
Standing timidly in the gloom
Under the golden gingko grove of home
Soaked in the rain last autumn?

Away from home this spring, from the train at dusk
I see an egret
Flap its ash-white wings
Soar among crimson clouds
And disappear!

獨酌

幾乎每次總是
在遠眺山下圍舞的燈火時
看見：一群斷翅的螢蟲
忙著，吞噬
被家書打翻的月光

有時難免想起
屋後那條潺潺流盪的溪河
沖破阻窄的隄防，青筋暴怒地
向源頭喊道：我不止是
一種，容器

1976

Drinking Alone

Nearly every time
The lights dance in a circle far down the hill
I see a group of fireflies
Busily, gulping down the
Moonlight spilled out of letters from home

Sometimes I can't help but recall
The purling creek behind the house
Breaking its narrow embankment, blue veined
Shouting in anger to its source: I can't be held by
A single container

山月

難免我會仰起多枝葉的手
承載妳
入夜傳裝時洗掉的容顏
據說前日雨後妳曾在
我們分別的小站徘徊

有種哀怨是與行色無關的
我靜靜梳理被風亂了的髮
並且只能說
自從我踏孤飛的翅膀走入野地
妳即已是一輪浪蕩的天空

1976

Mountain Moon

Unavoidably I raise my leafy hands
To carry your
Face washed away when clad in night
Someone said after the rain on the day before yesterday you
Lingered at the small station where we parted

There is a sadness that has nothing to do with departure
I quietly comb my hair disheveled by the wind
And can only say
Since I entered the wilds alone on the wing
You have been the overarching sky, dissipating

霧落

霧落下潮起一般地沖襲
那時仍舊聽到鏗鏘的斧金
響自逐漸隱退的山頭
啄啄地，彷彿空谷鳥鳴
悄悄地，霧侵佔了小村

霧落下黃昏一般地來臨
此時已經不見落漠的葉蔭
憐視開始發芽的小樹
緩慢地，我展讀父親遺下的信
迅速地，霧來窗裏讀我的眼睛

1977

The Fog Falls

The fog falls like the roiling, washing tide
Hearing at that time the striking of the axe
Sounding from the mountain top gradually dimming from view
Pecking like the birds calling in the empty valley
Quietly, the fog takes possession of the small village

The fog settles like dusk
The desolate shadows disappear then
Tenderly I look at a small tree, its buds bursting
Slowly, I read my dead father's letters
Quickly the fog is at the window to read my eyes.

森林

所有路巷皆婉轉在我們腳下罷了！
除了背負以及支持天空，
淚珠或者唾液，是無礙於站姿的。
生長，但尤其仰望，讓飛鳥自眼中奔出，
我們的足掌何等愛恨交錯地抓住泥土！

即令風窺雨伺雷嘲電怒，笑是無辜的，
我們仍可以戰鬥，用耳鬢廝磨。
如果門只一扇，開窗同樣見山，
是以我們挺腰直立，任令路巷紛紜，
至於論辯，大可交付激水與亂石。

1977

14

Forest

Gentle are the roads and lanes underfoot!
Aside from bearing up and supporting the sky,
Tears or spit, have no impact on standing upright.
Growing, especially looking up, to let the birds fly from our eyes,
How our soles grasp the soil with a mixture of love and hate!

Watched by wind and rain or taunted by thunder and lightning,
Laughter is innocent, still we can fight, on intimate terms together.
If the door is a single leaf, the mountain can be seen the same
          by opening a window,
We stand upright, let the roads and lanes be many and confused,
As for debate, hand it over to the rushing water and stone riprap.

草根

即使是再莽撞再劇烈的剷掘，
我也會柔曲著體幹忍受。
原不善於面對烈日陰雨的，
你踢走了我藏身的泥沙，
還留我一地石礫灰白……

所以只要晚露在闃闇中降臨，
我便默默伸出觸鬚，覓尋泥土，
從事另一次紮根，艱苦而愉
悅的旅行。如你再度來到，唇
角捺著一撇諷嘲，我歉然還你
媚綠的微笑

1977

Grass Roots

Uprooted all the more impetuously and violently
Still I'll softly bend and bear it. Though never
Good at facing the scorching sun and excess rain
You kick away my sheltering sand and soil,
Leave me a patch of gray gravel . . .

So, only if the evening dew comes in the dim darkness
Will I then silently send my runners forth, searching the soil,
Once more to take root, a hard and pleasant journey.
If you come again mouthing taunts,
I'll flash my charming green smile in return.

心事

浮雲把陰霾的顏面埋入
迴映碧樹蒼空的小湖
小湖又把圈圈圈不住的皺紋
隨風交給游魚去處理了
所謂心事是楊柳繞著小湖徘徊

逝去的昨夜挽留著將來的明天
落葉則在霧靄裏翩翩飄墜
而悲哀與喜樂永遠如此沈默
只教湖上橋的倒影攔下
倒影裏魚和葉相見的驚訝

1978

My Cares

Floating clouds sink their gloomy faces
In a small pond reflecting verdant trees and blue sky
And the pond sends the circling ripples with the wind
To swimming fish
My cares are the willows pacing around the shore

Departing night urges tomorrow to stay
Leaves flutter down through the mist
But joy and sorrow remain silent forever
There, in the reflection of the bridge railing
The surprise encounter of the fish and the leaves

種籽

除非毅然離開靠託的美麗花冠
我只能俯聞到枝枒枯萎的聲音
一切溫香、蜂蝶和昔日，都要
隨風飄散。除非拒絕綠葉掩護
我才可以等待泥土爆破的心驚

但擇居山陵便緣慳於野原空曠
棲止海濱，則失落溪澗的洗滌
天與地之間，如是廣闊而狹仄
我飄我飛我蕩，僅為尋求固定
適合自己，去縶根繁殖的土地

1978

Seed

I'll just stoop, listening as the twigs and branches wither
Unless I resolutely break from this beautiful and reliant corolla
As all the fragrances, the bees, the butterflies, and the yesterdays
Scattered by the wind. Only by rejecting the protective
        camouflage of green leaves
Will I be able to wait for the soil's fearsome blast

But if I choose to dwell on a mountain slope,
        then the open wilds will be closed to me
If I settle at the seashore, then I'll lose the cleansing stream
Between heaven and earth, so broad yet so narrow
I drift, I fly, I float to find a suitable place
To settle, take root, and be fruitful

秋辭

葉子攀不住枯黯的枝枒
紛紛奔向清晨微寒的潭心
有人打傘自多露的湖畔走過
只聽見右側林中跳下一顆
松子，驚聲喊道

你就這樣來了嗎？漣漪
和回聲都流連在空盪的水面上
一些浮萍忽然站了起來
留下山的倒影明晰地吻著雨後
蔚藍的天空，而秋是深得更深了

1979

Autumn Words

No longer can the leaves cling to withered limbs
Falling in droves they speed to the heart of the cold lake at dawn
Someone with an umbrella walks the dew-drenched shore
From the forest all that is heard is a falling
Pine cone, a startled cry

Is this how you arrive? Ripples
And echoes linger over the quiet water
The duckweed suddenly parts
Leaving the mountain's reflection kissing
The blue rain-washed sky, and autumn is deeper

立場

你問我立場，沈默地
我望著天空的飛鳥而拒絕
答腔，在人群中我們一樣
呼吸空氣，喜樂或者哀傷
站著，且在同一塊土地上

不一樣的是眼光，我們
同時目睹馬路兩旁，眾多
腳步來來往往。如果忘掉
不同路向，我會答覆你
人類雙腳所踏，都是故鄉

1984

Stand

You ask where I stand, in silence
I look up at the birds in the sky and refuse
To reply, among the crowd we breathe the same
Air, standing we experience happiness and sadness
But on this same piece of ground we

See things differently, at the same time
We see the crowds passing by
On both sides of the street. If we forget our
Different directions, I will answer you
Home is where humanity treads.

制服

他們穿著一致的服裝，擺盪
一致的手臂，邁出一致的步伐
走在春草茸茸的路上，滿意地
把眉毛、嘴唇、肩膀靠攏成
水平線──仔細丈量沈靜的野原

甚至連風也不敢咳嗽。他們
砍伐了自高自大的樹木，修剪
枝葉分歧的花草，最後一致
仰首搖頭──身為地上的園丁
當然制服不了空中化的雲朵

1984

Uniform

They all wear the same uniform, their arms
All swing in unison, they all march to the same step
On a road of lush spring grass; they are content
To close ranks, their eyebrows, mouths, and shoulders
Forming a line to carefully measure the silent plain

Even the wind dares not cough. They
Chop down the conceited trees, prune away
Leafy branches and flowers; finally they all
Look up and shake their heads, for naturally, as
dressers and keepers of this earthly garden, they
Cannot force uniformity on the clouds in the sky.

寒流

有人與我爭執，關於民謠史的
演變，主張某些歌謠根本是
殘花，應該從園中徹底清除
他的意見是對的。寒風來時
凡虛假與脆弱的總會背枝離葉

背枝離葉是事實，我們親眼
目見，很多花豔麗於瞬間
飄零呢，在永遠。他的意見
冷酷如寒流，可能風行於瞬間
卻昧於永遠──關於史的演變

1984

Cold Current

Someone argued with me about the historical development of
Folk songs, viewing some of them basically as
Withered flowers, which should be thoroughly eliminated
He is right. When a cold wind comes, the false and
The fragile are always removed from the branches and leaves

Being removed from the branches and leaves is a fact, we have
Personally seen many flowers resplendent but for a twinkling
Then fade and fall for all time. His opinion
Cruel as a cold current, perhaps fashionable for a twinkling
But forever ignorant—about historical development

Dialect Poems

阿爹的飯包

每一日早起時，天猶未光
阿爹就帶著飯包
騎著舊鐵馬，離開厝
出去溪埔替人搬沙石

每一暝阮攏在想
阿爹的飯包到底什麼款
早頓阮和阿兄食包仔配豆乳
阿爹的飯包起碼也有一粒蛋
若無安怎替人搬沙石

有一日早起時，天猶烏烏
阮偷偷走入去灶腳內，掀開
阿爹的飯包：無半粒蛋
三條菜脯，蕃薯籤參飯

1976

Dad's Lunchbox

Every morning, Dad got up before the sun
He took his lunchbox and
Rode his old bike to the stream bed
To haul gravel

Every night I wondered
What was in Dad's lunchbox
Every morning my brother and I ate our fill
       of stuffed buns and soy milk
Dad surely had an egg in his lunchbox
Otherwise, how could he haul gravel

One morning when it was still dark
I got up and tiptoed to the kitchen
There was no egg in Dad's lunchbox
Just sweet-potato rice, and pickled radish

議員仙仔無在厝

議員仙仔無佇厝
一個月前為着村民的利益
他就出門去縣城努力
道路拓寬以後交通便利
工廠一間一間起大家大賺錢

議員仙仔一向真飽學
聽講彼日在議會發威
先是罵縣老爺無夠力飯桶
續落去笑局長是龜孫仔
議員仙仔是官虎頂頭的大官虎

當初這票投了實在無不對
不但賺煙賺錢賺味素
而且如今找議員仙仔同款真照顧
東一句王兄西一句李弟
握一個手任何問題攏無問題

可惜議員仙仔無在厝
新起的一間工廠放廢水
田裡的稻仔攏總死死掉
可惜議員仙仔一個月前就出門去
爭取道路拓寬工廠起好大家大賺錢

1976

His Honor, Mr. Assemblyman, Is Not at Home

His honor, Mr. Assemblyman, is not at home
He went to the county seat a month ago
On behalf of the people
After the road is widened, traffic will improve
Factories will spring up and everyone will get rich

His honor, Mr. Assemblyman, really knows a thing or two
It's said when he wielded power at the Assembly
First he called the county boss a useless piece of . . .
Then laughing, he swore at a government official
His honor, Mr. Assemblyman, is top dog in a dog-eat-dog world

He was the right choice
We got cigarettes, money, and good food
Nobody can take better care of us than
       his honor, Mr. Assemblyman
Here a word, there a handshake with a pal
And everything is taken care of

Too bad his honor, Mr. Assemblyman is not at home
One of the new factories dumps waste water
Which kills the rice in the fields
Too bad his honor, Mr. Assemblyman left a month ago
To fight to have the road widened
After more factories are built
       We'll all get rich

村長伯仔欲造橋

為著庄裡的交通收成的運送
猶有囡仔的教育
溪沙同款算未完的理由
村長伯仔每一家每一戶撞門
講是造橋重要愛造橋

村長伯仔實在了不起
舊年裝的路燈今年會發光的存一半
今年修的水管舊年也已經修過兩三遍
只有溪埔雖然無溪水也愛有一條橋
有橋了後都市人會來庄裡就發達
造橋重要收成運送也順利

造橋確實重要無者庄裡就無腳
計程車會得過不過小包車想欲過不敢過
咱的庄裡觀光資本有十成便利無半成
造橋重要請村民支持這亦不是為我自己
雖然我有一臺金龜車，橋若無造
同款和各位父老步輪過溪埔

The Village Chief Wants to Build a Bridge

The village chief wants to build a bridge
To make it easier for people of the village to transport crops
And educating the children
With more reasons than grains of sand in the riverbed
The village chief goes door to door
Talking about the importance of the bridge
        the need to build a bridge

The village chief is really something
Of the street lights he had installed last year
        only half still shine this year
The water pipes he's repairing this year
        have been repaired two or three times before
And though there's no water in the river
        he still wants to build a bridge
For once there's a bridge the city folks'll come
        and the village will develop
A bridge is important and it'll be easier
        to transport the crops

Building a bridge is really important
        otherwise the village will be backward
The cabs and trucks dare not pass
There's lots of money to be had from sightseeing
        in our village but it's inconvenient
Building a bridge is important, please support it
        I'm not in this for myself
Though I have a nice car until the bridge is built
I'll walk across the riverbed like the rest of you

村長伯仔講話算話
每一日自溪埔彼邊來庄裡走縱
為著全庄的交通村民的利便
他將彼臺金龜車鎖佇車庫內
村長伯仔講是橋若無造他就不開鎖
哎！造橋確實重要愛造橋

1976

The village chief means what he says
Every day he has to cross the riverbed to get to the village
For village transportation and the convenience of the villagers
He has locked his car in the garage
And says there it'll stay until the bridge is built
O! building a bridge is really important we have to build a bridge

食頭路

食人的頭路真艱苦
透早起來得出門
搧冷風，等公車
搖頭踩腳看手錶
苦苦等，苦苦看
公車擠著人已經昏倒一大半

食人的頭路真痛苦
每日上班得打拼
看頂司，賠面色
喝東不敢向西行
苦苦做，苦苦爬
月給領到人已經減活幾仔歲

食人的頭路真辛苦
不時透暝得
加班聽鐘聲，算時間
一分一秒有夠慢
苦苦算，苦苦等
日頭看到人已經腳手懶懶

1982

Nine to Five

This job has got me down
Up early to stand in the cold
Waiting for the bus, shake your head
Stamp your feet, look at your watch
Wait, wait, wait
The crowded bus nearly makes you faint

This job is a pain
Working hard every day
Gotta watch the boss's moods
Don't dare cross him
Just work, work, work
Killing yourself for
a few bucks each month

This job has got me down
Sometimes you've gotta work
till late at night
Listening to the clock, counting
the minutes
Time drags on and on and on
When the sun comes up
you're ready for bed

A Miscellany

夜過小站聞雨

越過廣垠的原野無聲的夜
翻過暗黑的山巒無語的夜
靜靜落下是天空陰冷的臉
徐徐逼來是海洋鹹濕的淚

海洋的淚躲進窗中那臉上
天空的臉逃入眼前那燈內
燈在夜裏徐徐翻過那山巒
夜在燈裏靜靜越過那原野

靜靜越過小站陰冷的牆垣
徐徐翻過小站鹹濕的簷榭
列列廊柱閃若無情的刀影
幽幽落葉飄似旅人的歎喟

歎喟迅即被黑夜的嘴吞噬
刀影仍舊隨細雨的睫揮舞
燈在夜裏不屈地掙掙昇起
夜在燈裏委曲地徐徐離去

1977

Passing through a Small Station at Night, Listening to the Rain

Through broad fields on a silent night, I pass
Cross dark mountains on a speechless night
What quietly falls is the cold and gloomy face of the sky
What slowly approaches are the sea's salty tears

The sea's tears hide on a face in the window
The sky's face flees into the lamp before the eyes
The lamp slowly crosses mountains in the night
The night in the lamp quietly passes through fields

Quietly I pass the cold and gloomy walls of the small station
Pass the salty wet eaves of the small station
Columns in a row flash by like the shadows of merciless blades
The dark falling leaves float like a traveler's sighs

The sighs are immediately swallowed up by the night
Still the shadows of brandished blades descend with the drizzle's lashes
Quietly the lamp rises, unbowed in the night
Slowly the night tortuously departs from inside the lamp

歲月跟著

歲月跟著馬蹄不停地跑
滴答的秒針是蹄的聲音
馳過了三月的青翠森林
馳過了兒童粲亮的眼睛

歲月跟著犁耙沈穩地耕
雍容的分針是犁的鋒刃
翻閱著六月的綠色大地
翻閱著你我粗糙的掌紋

歲月跟著貓爪偷偷地移
緩慢的時針是貓的腳步
躡走了九月的天光雲影
躡走了老人眼角的水霧

歲月跟著永恒輪迴地繞
圓柔的鐘面是生命的枷
熟透的花果在十二月凋
土底的種籽正開始抽芽

1978

46

Time Follows

Time follows, running with a horse's hoofs, never stopping
The tick-tock of the second hand is the hoof beats
Speeding through the green forest of March
Speeding through a child's bright eyes

Time follows the plow's steady progress
The stately minute hand is the ploughshare
Glancing at the green earth of June
Glancing at the coarse lines in our palms

Time follows the stealthy steps of a cat
The slow hour hand is the cat's padding
Treading through the light and clouds of September
Treading through the mist in an old person's eyes

Time follows, turning with the eternal cycle
The clock's round face is the cangue of life
Overripe fruit withers in December
Seeds in the soil just begin to sprout

菊嘆

所有等待，只為金線菊
微笑著在寒夜裡徐徐綻放
像林中的落葉輕輕，飄下
那種招呼，美如水聲
又微帶些風的怨嘆
讓人從蕨類咬住的小徑
驚見澄黃的月光，還有
傍晚樵夫遺下的柴枝
冷冷鬱結著的
褪了色的幽淒

走過總是垂髮低頭，故意
是裝不來的，林外的溪水
緊緊攀著草夜的幾滴淚
此刻在風中，瓦解了
妳問我浮萍的邏輯
那就是吧，露珠向大地
沉墜的輕唷。而菊
尤其金線菊是耐於等待的
寒冬過了就是春天
我用一生來等妳的展顏

1978

Chrysanthemum Sigh

All the waiting, just for golden-thread chrysanthemums
Smiling, slowly coming into bloom on a cold night
Softly as the leaves falling in the forest, falling
A greeting, as beautiful as the sound of water
Along with a little anger of wind
Let the people on the fern-gripped path
Catch sight of the yellow moonlight with surprise, along with
The firewood left behind by the wood cutter at dusk
Cold and pent up
The faded desolation
Always with head and hair hanging down, playing
Dumb, the stream beyond the forest
Tightly clings to the tears of the grassy night
Dissolving now amid the wind
You ask me about the duckweed's logic
That's it, the sigh of the dew on the earth. And the mums
Especially the golden-thread chrysanthemum must patiently wait
For spring to come after winter passes
I'll wait my whole life for your smile to unfold

泥土與花

——語言與詩的思考

花在風和日麗中飽滿
而奕奕地開放了，以妖冶
而嫵媚的臉顏仰望青空
睨視腳下的泥土，並且招展
她一貫強調的美學
在恆溫的氣候中，向曠野
大聲宣佈：所謂象徵
是她身上一切瓣一切蕊
所謂純粹是，不染塵埃
遠離泥土、通向天堂的梯階

泥土默然，木訥地負載著花
及其驕狂，一句話也不說
只是夜裏拼命蒐集雨露
供花日裏大加揮霍
只是日裏努力聚合養料
護衛不斷向體內進逼的
根鬚，讓花有所吸收
無所謂純粹，無所謂超越
只是粗糙、駁雜而堅穩

花愈豔麗，泥土愈加低頭
花在炫耀誇張下日形憔悴
泥土因容納而日漸肥沃
當狂風疾雨一夕驟至
瓣與蕊紛紛背離了枝頭
投入始生與歸宿的泥土
從頭學習在塵埃中生活

The Soil and the Flower

The flower bud swells in the gentle breeze and bright sunlight
Gracefully opens, her bewitchingly attractive
Face looks up at the blue sky
She looks suspiciously at the soil beneath her feet,
      and flaunts the aesthetics she has always emphasized
In a perpetually warm climate, she announces
To the open fields: the so-called symbols
Are her petals and pistil
So-called purity is a ladder to heaven
Unspoiled and rising above the dirt

The soil silently and honestly supports the flower
And her wild arrogance, not a word does it say
All night long it madly collects the dew
To provide her with all the more during the day
All day long it diligently gathers nutrients
And never stops guarding her roots
With no thoughts about purity and transcendence
It is rough and impure but firm and stable

The more beautiful the flower,
      the lower sinks the soil's head
Showiness and exaggeration make the flower
      grow thin and wane
The soil bears all and slowly grows fat
When a violent storm arrives
Petals and pistil fall from the stem
Joining the soil that gave her life and home
Learning to live once again in the dirt

在綻放與凋謝間，花似死
而實生；而在施與受中
泥土依舊木然地迎接
另一朵花的誕生及其喧鬧

1982

Between blooming, withering, seemingly dead
But still alive; and between giving and receiving
The soil, as usual, silently welcomes
The birth of another flower and its noisy clamor

發現□□

□□被發現
在一九二〇年出版的
多份發黃而枯裂的新聞紙上

在歷史嘲弄的唇邊
□□業已湮滅
啄木鳥也啄不出什麼
□□之中
空空 洞洞

在她飄移的裙緣
□□靜候填充
駭浪怒潮左右窺伺
□□ □□
懵懵 懂懂

在有限的四方框內
空空洞洞的 □□
□□ 葡萄牙水手叫她 Formosa
□□ 荷蘭賜她 Zeelandia 之名
□□ 鄭成功填入明都平安
□□ 大清在其上設府而隸福建
□□ 棄民在此成立民主國
□□ 日本種入大和魂
□□ 現在據說是中國不可分割的肉
在無數的符號之中
懵懵 懂懂的 □□

Discovering □□

□ □ was discovered
In several newspapers from 1920
Yellowed and disintegrating

On the mocking lips of history
□ □ has already been destroyed
A woodpecker cannot peck anything
Out of □ □
Empty void

On the fluttering hem of her skirt
□ □ waits quietly to be filled in
Fearful billows and angry currents wait and watch
       Left and right
□ □ □ □
Muddled ignorant

In a confining frame
Empty void □ □
□ □ The Portugese sailors called her Formosa
□ □ the Dutch bestowed the name Zeelandia on her
□ □ Zheng Chenggong filled in "Peace, the capital of Ming"
□ □ the Qing established a prefecture subordinate to
       Fujian Province
□ □ a people abandoned established a republic
□ □ Japan transplanted "Great Japan" here
□ □ now she is said to be an inseperable part of China
Among so many signifiers
Muddled ignorant □ □

什麼都是的□□
什麼都不是的□□
猶似紅檜，在濃濃霧中
找不到踏腳的土地
所有的鳥競相插上羽翅
所有的獸爭逐彼此足跡
發現□□成為一種趣味
尋找□□變做閒來無事的遊戲

□□被複製
在一九九一年冬付梓的
以及部份被付之一炬的
選舉公報中
□□被發現
在□□圍起來的□□中
在空洞的□□裡
□□以□□為名
終至於連□□也找不到了

1992

56

□ □ is everything
□ □ is nothing
Like a Formosa Cypress in thick fog
Unable to find ground on which to stand
All the birds vie to nest their feathery wings
All the beasts contend to leave their tracks
Discovering □ □ has become a form of leisure
Searching for □ □ has become an idle pastime

□ □ was duplicated
In an election bulletin
Published in the winter of 1991
Part of which was consigned to flames
□ □ was discovered
In the □ □ surrounded by □ □
In the empty □ □
□ □ was called by the name of □ □
Until finally even □ □ could no longer be found

亂

在靜寂的夜中醒過來來
醒過來的夜喧譁著

墨藍的天空隱藏迷幻的紅
淺綠的窗簾飄搖虛空的白
鐘擺彷彿也被嚇呆了
所有指針都反向逃竄

沈默的夜，沈默的張狂
囚車烏黑，滿載叛徒顛簸前行
群眾以白眼，魚肚一般翻破了天
血雨灑落子彈犁過的田
一堵廢牆依舊顫抖，在灰瓦下
孩童躲在沙包間找尋太陽
雞鴨，為地盤吵架
夢中被棄的小村，偷空打了一個小盹

從靜寂的夜中醒過來
醒過來的夜回味夢中的夢
分不清是金邊市郊即景
還是波士尼亞邊區北愛爾蘭麥格賀拉斐特鎮
分不清是西藏山區伊拉克南界
或者厄利垂亞農村約翰尼斯堡城外
有些國家醒著有些國家睡了有些國家
未醒未睡半醒半睡腥紅著雙眼
在靜寂的夜中狂亂
在狂亂的夜中靜寂
髮眼鼻耳舌頸胸腹腰肚手臂腿腳趾
都攪在一塊兒給砲火帶走了

Chaos

Waking on a quiet night
Awake, the night clamors

The blue-black sky conceals a hallucinatory red
The light green curtains an empty white
The pendulum stops in fright
Reversed, the clock hands all point to flight

Silent night, dissipation in silence
The dark police van filled with rebels jolts along
People look on with disdain as the sky turns fish-belly bright
A bloody rain falls on fields plowed by bullets
As usual, a broken wall trembles under gray roof tiles
Children seek the sun amid sandbags
Chickens and ducks squabble over territory
The dream-forsaken village steals a wink of shuteye

Waking on a quiet night
Awake, the night recalls a dream in a dream
Unable to tell if it's Phnom Pehn and its suburbs
Or the Bosnian border, Magherafelt in Northern Ireland
Unable to tell if it's mountainous Tibet, southern Iraq
Or Eritrea Village outside Johannesburg
Some nations wake, some nations sleep, some nations
Are red-eyed, between waking and sleeping
Frenzy on a quiet night
Quiet on a frenzied night
Hair, eyes, nose, neck chest, abdomen, waist, belly,
        hands, arms, legs, feet, toes
All jumbled together, obliterated by artillery fire

這夜也以另一種臉顏沈默著
在曼谷在紐約在巴黎在莫斯科在上海在台北
愛滋通過血水交容滋生愛的共同體
罌粟大麻植床在人類的體膚上
狂歡舔上都會男女乾渴的唇間
飢餓寫入窮鄉孩童的骨頭
核能電廠獰笑，等待下一回的奔放
臭氧層苦澀的傷口，百無聊賴地，擺著
在靜寂的夜中醒過來
世界洲界國界人界皆已泯滅
只剩皮膚與皮膚競逐顏色

在靜寂的夜中醒過來的夜喧譁著
醒是夢，夢死也醉生，醉後還得醒
和平夢，夢戰爭，戰爭夢和平
積木一樣，隨意堆疊
亂，也隨意堆疊
積木一樣溫順沈默的我們
在政客軍頭的遊戲中
被集合被解散被撿拾被棄置被敲打被命令
被編號被設籍被上色被分類被排列被界定
在夜的某個區位中
在亂的某個經緯上
在我們自己也搞不清楚的某個夢裡
我們堅決相信可以夢見黎明

醒過來，自靜寂的夢中
這個世界用亂建構了邏輯
愛與恨以對立的鬥爭相互取暖
在夢的狂亂中
我們因為沈睡，錯過黎明
至於鐘擺

The silent night has another face
In Bangkok, New York, Paris, Moscow, Shanghai, Taipei
AIDS transmits through blood and fluids of the collective body
The human body is a garden bed for poppies and marijuana
Metropolitan men and women revel, licking parched lips
Famine is written in the bones of the impoverished children
The nuclear power plant laughs malignantly, waiting for the next meltdown
The painful wound in the ozone layer, bored, situated
Waking on a quiet night
Vanished are the world, continents, nations, people and their boundaries
Leaving only the skins to vie for color

On a quiet night, night wakes and clamors
Wakefulness is a dream, dreaming in death or drinking in life,
after getting drunk, you still have to sober up
Dream of peace, dream of war, war dreams of peace
Like toy building blocks, piled as you please
Chaos, too, piles up as you please
Docile and silent, we are like toy building blocks
In the games of politicians and generals
Assembled we are, dispersed, collected, abandoned, beaten, ordered
Numbered, registered, graded, colored, categorized, arranged, defined
In some area of the night
At some longitude and latitude of chaos
In some dream we cannot comprehend
We firmly believe that we can dream of dawn

Awakened from a quiet dream
The world uses slipshod logic
Love and hate seek mutual warmth in their perpetual fight
In the frenzy of a dream
Sleeping soundly, we miss the dawn
As for the pendulum
It's still there where it ought to be

仍擺在該擺的地方
在靜寂的夜中
動也不動

1993

On a quiet night
Swinging
Yet not swinging

山路

在風中穿過箭竹草原
在風中穿過冷杉林
只有斷嶺殘山從雲霧中探出
與我們驚喜相覷
一路相陪是玉山圓柏與杜鵑
開在裸岩走過的盡處
陽光潛入細碎的林葉間
藍色的天俯視大水窟、大關山和馬博拉斯
桀敖不馴的脊背
這山路，在群峰中尋覓傲骨

這山路，在群峰中望向高處
酒紅朱雀拍擊薄雪草的翅身
蒼綠挺拔，是二葉松擎起整座天空
遠處有瀑水為鍊，輝耀山的胸膛
欲離還留的雲霧
以一襲薄紗勾引暗戀的山巒
山路來到此處
濁水、高屏和秀姑巒都找到了源頭
海峽在左，大洋在右
台灣從海上升起在玉山之顛放歌

2002

Mountain Road

We pass over a plain of arrow bamboo in the wind
We pass through a fir forest in the wind
Only broken crags and rugged ridges poke through the clouds
Looking at each other and at us with surprise and delight
The big cypress trees of Jade Mountain escort us all the way
   and the azaleas
Bloom to the farthest point of naked rocks
The sunlight seeps down through mottled foliage
The blue sky looks down upon Dashuiku, and the intractable
   backs of
Daguan Mountain and Mabolasi Mountain
Among the peaks this rutted road seeks loftiness

Among the peaks this rutted road looks to the heights
A wine-red rose finch wings through the screening snow grass
The two-needle pines stand green and straight, holding up
   the whole sky
In the distance, a waterfall is a chain, shining on the breast
   of the mountain
The lingering cloud-mist
Like a concealing veil, tempts the mountains with secret love
Where the mountain road leads
The Cho-shui, the Kao-ping and the Hsiu-ku-luan rivers all find
   their source
To the left: the Straits
To the right: the Pacific
Taiwan rises from the sea to sing at the peak of Jade Mountain

The Four Seasons
[1986]

立春

星星正細數著小村的巷弄
燈火卻已逐一走進夢中
幾聲蛙鼓打破了天地
沈默，有人在靜夜裡咳嗽
伴著風，與竹葉悉索細說
連小溪也不甘──不甘示弱
　　　這土地曾經蕭瑟
　　　愛情也被凍縮了
有人夜半驚坐，瞧見星光
潛入窗內，在殘稿上思索

黑暗，許是星星發光的理由
寒冷，則被愛情當做瑟縮的藉口
花皆凋落，塵泥卻獲得
溫熱。而溫熱是通過冷漠
潺潺不斷的水流，經土地
逐歲月，澆灑殘稿之上
未竟的空格。有人
半夜驚坐，星光漸稀
向沈寂的冬夜
溪水擦亮了春火

Beginning of Spring

The stars count the village lanes and alleys
One by one the lights move closer to dream
Drumming frogs break the silence of Heaven and Earth
Someone coughs in the night
The wind blows, bamboo leaves whisper
Even the stream seems to pause
This land was made desolate by the cold
Love, too, was frozen
Startled, someone sits up and watches the starlight
Slip through the window and pour over a manuscript

Perhaps the stars shine because of the darkness
And love shrinks away because of the cold
The flowers have fallen but the soil warms
Warmth passes through the cold, purling stream
Over the land, in pursuit of time
Watering the empty spaces in the manuscript
At midnight someone sits up
The starlight slowly grows dim
On a silent winter night
The stream brightens the fire of spring

雨水

一路隨防波堤快步跑來的
是海峽層層推湧的白
添一些波光，冷冷襲入
港的胸膛。遠處有
三兩漁船，纏鬥著風浪
烏魚群躲避著羅網
漁人張開勁健的雙手
撐出膀上汗與鹽的光芒
暖流這時正一寸一寸撫過岩岸
黑潮不捨，由南北上

黑潮沖激，沿島的東域
帶來漁穫，也攜來暖和
但海上並不溫柔，風慫恿雲
雲呼喚雨，雨可不客氣
一霎時撞進港的臂灣裡
船也陸續，馬達啟動
逐防波堤而來。前推後湧
是春天上陸的消息
冬，就此解凍
雨水正豐

The Rains

Rows of white waves surge in from the Straits
With light they dash in
Along the breakwater, coldly attacking
The heart of the harbor. Far from shore
Two or three fishing boats struggle amid wind and wave
Schools of mullet flee the nets
The fishermen flex their strong hands
Their shoulders shine with salt and sweat
The warm ocean current brings relief to the rocky shore
The Kuroshio Current does not give, it rushes

North along the east coast
Bringing a plenitude of fish and warmth
While churning the sea. The wind brings clouds
The clouds bring rain, violent squalls
That burst through the harbor's arms
The boats continue on, engines chugging
Coming in along the breakwater, bustling
With news of spring's Arrival to land
Winter begins to thaw
Rain water is at its most abundant

驚蟄

寒意自昨夜起逐步撤退
清晨進駐林間的一隊鳥聲
把微曦與樹影咬成起落的音階
久潮牆角，忽然暈染開來
破窗過訪的陽光，靜靜
溫慰著瑟縮的鋤犁。北風
向西，一波波湧溢
靄靄氣息。屋舍昂然抖擻
泥土中，蟄蟲正待開門探頭
隨蛺蝶，我入園中遊走

一似去年，田犁碌碌耙梳土地
汗與血還是要向新泥生息
鷺鷥輕踩牛背，蚯蚓翻滾
在田畝中，我播種
在世世代代不斷翻耕的悲喜裡
放眼是遠山近樹翩飛新綠
昨夜寒涼，且遣澗水漂離
我耕作，但為這塊美麗大地
期待桃花應聲開放
當雷霆破天，轟隆直下

Waking of Insects

Last night the cold began its slow retreat
This morning bird song invades the forest
Scaled to match the light and shadow at dawn
The sunlight breaks through the window
To visit long-damp corners, silently
Warming shovels and plows. The north wind
Turns westward, surging
Clouds in the sky.
Hibernating insects prepare to emerge from the soil
I wander in the garden, following butterflies

Like last year, the plows are busy turning earth
Sweat and blood are worked into the new soil
Egrets perch on the backs of buffalos,
        earthworms wriggle
I plow and sow the fields
Of joy and sadness cultivated for generations
The distant green hills and nearby trees fill my eyes
It was cold last night, but the mountain stream is flowing
I plow this lovely land
Waiting for peach tree blossoms to echo
As thunder shakes down from the sky

春分

彷彿循環著的日與月
我在東，你在西
分別擁有一半的世界
彷彿綻開著的花或蕊
你是桃，我是李
各自描繪不同的畫頁
彷彿遠隔著的南與北
我上山，你下海
埋頭譜寫相異的音階
背靠春天，孤獨使我們掉淚

彷彿相生著的樹與葉
我盤根，你蔚綠
一起接受陽光和雨水
彷彿併聯著的路與街
你走縱，我走橫
相互提供生命的圖繪
彷彿舞踊著的蜂或蝶
我在左，你在右
共同吸取天地的精粹
面向春風，我們分頭而雙飛

Vernal Equinox

Like the circling sun and moon
We each possess half the world
You the west, and I the east
Like the blossom and the bursting bud
We each paint a different picture
You the peach, and I the pear
As distant as opposing compass points
We compose songs to different scales
I ascend a mountain, and you go down to the sea
Spring is behind us, and loneliness
is the reason for our tears

With the essential unity of root and leaf
We absorb sunlight and water
I am the tangled roots, and you the lush foliage
Like a grid of roads and lanes
We provide each other with a map of life
You walk the vertical, and I the horizontal
Like dancing bees and butterflies
We imbibe the essences of the universe
I am on the right, you are on the left
Taking flight on a spring breeze, we go separate ways

清明

昨夜的雨仍然低迴
在今晨的路上，柳枝
披掛在河岸。河的兩端
生與死從橋上來來往往
昨夜的雨，仍然低迴在今晨
行人紛紛的路上，愛與恨
相錯而過橋的兩端
柳枝披掛在渾濛的河岸
薄霧薄霧，俯首水面
悲哀和快樂都已茫然

低迴在今晨，昨夜的雨
昨夜的死生悲喜，仍然在
路上，行人紛紛柳枝
紛紛，穿過薄霧走過河岸
一枝小草吮著一點露
仍然低迴在今晨的路上
昨夜的雨，不歇不息
紛紛打過行人的髮際
露珠露珠，懸垂草葉
最難分辨是雨水或眼淚

Tomb Sweeping

Last night's rain still falls on
The road this morning, willow branches
Droop over the river banks. From both shores
Life and death shuttle across the bridge
Last night's rain is still here this morning
On the bustling road, love and hate
Miss, crossing the bridge
Willows weep along the mist-shrouded banks
Leaning over the water
Joy and sorrow fade

Last night's rain is still here this morning,
Last night's death and life, joy and sorrow are still on
The road, thronging, people pass
Through the mist to the other shore
A blade of grass absorbs a drop of dew
Last night's rain
Hangs over the road this morning
Falls on people's heads
Dewdrops on the leaves of grass
Rain or tears?

穀雨

我們從丘陵的眉間
醒過來，從霧的眼波裡
醒過來。這時已是暮春
三月，也在綠的盛粧中
醒過來。陽光行過相思林
給探頭的我們以澄黃
以及微笑。我們是綠的族群
二三百年來就站在褐的土地
蘊釀同陽光一樣，一樣黃澄
撲鼻的甘醇與芳香

向更古遠的年代，西元
七六〇頃，隱居在苕溪
大唐的逸士陸羽低頭試著
叫醒我們：茶者，南方之嘉木也
來自南方的我們，三百年來
站在這島上，因四時節氣
有不同的色澤，如今在雨前
我們醒過來，從丘陵的眉間
　　醒過來，從霧的眼波裡
大聲叫著：茶，性喜向陽

Grain Rain

We awaken on the brows of the hills
Behind the eyelids of
The fog. It's already March,
Late spring, and we also awaken
To lush green. Sunlight walks through
The forest of love
Coloring our budding heads with pure yellow
And a smile. A green tribe
We have stood on this brown land for centuries
Fermenting like the yellow sun

Sweet and fragrant as wine
Long ago during the high Tang
The hermit Lu Yi looked down and tried
To awaken us—"Tea, fair plant of the south."
Native to the south, we have stood on
This island for centuries, changing color
With the seasons. Today, we awaken before
The rain comes, we awaken on the brows of
The hills, behind the eyelids of the fog
We shout: "Tea likes the sun."

立夏

從眼前行過平原的
不是低垂的雲，是風
呼叫青翠的稻禾，呼叫
一路列隊的木棉，呼叫
燕子，銜著新泥到農舍簷間
從平原拂向山邊的
不是綿密的雨，昨夜
雨已經帶著春天回去
夏，正像今朝的木棉
站在平原上綻開了花的紅艷

從山邊推過峰頂的
不是茫漠的霧，是綠
喚醒相思松柏與杉林，喚醒
峰頂初昇的太陽，喚醒
新竹，低頭俯瞰廣袤大地
從峰頂指向天際的
不是黯淡的月，今晨
月已經跟著春天隱去
夏，正是初昇的太陽
站在峰頂上綻放出光的溫熱

Beginning of Summer

The wind passes over the plain
Not the low clouds
It calls to the jade-green rice plants, calls
To the rows of kapoks, calls
To the swallows carrying fresh mud to farmhouse eaves
It's not the drizzling rain that was
Pushed from plain to mountains, last night
The rain carried away spring
Summer is like the red kapoks
Blooming on the plain this morning

The green flows over the peaks
Not the fog
It awakens the pines, the cypresses and the firs of love, awakens
The newly risen sun, awakens
The new bamboo looking down on the vast earth
It's not the moon that has risen directly over the peaks, the moon
Departed with spring this morning
Summer is like the newly risen sun
Standing above the peaks bursting with warm light

小滿

一隻青蛙撲通跳下池塘
打破樹上烏鴉的睡意
荷葉跟著驚顫幾下
水面的漣漪一圈圈
把靜寂擴散了出去
蓮花孤獨地坐著
燠悶的夏日午后
連雲們都懶得來相陪
一行螞蟻運搬著麵包屑
頗富節奏地走過土丘

頗富節奏地走過土丘
一行螞蟻運搬著麵包屑
連雲們都懶得來相陪
燠悶的夏日午后
蓮花孤獨地坐著
把靜寂擴散了出去
水面的漣漪一圈圈
荷葉跟著驚顫幾下
打破樹上烏鴉的睡意
一隻青蛙撲通跳下池塘

Lesser Fullness of Grain

Splash! A frog jumps in the pond
Startling the drowsy crows in the trees
The lily pads tremble
Ripples ring outward over the water
Spreading tranquility
The lotus sits alone
On this stifling summer afternoon
Even the clouds are loath to appear
In a column, ants carry bread crumbs
Walking rhythmically over the bumpy ground

Walking rhythmically over the bumpy ground
In a column, ants carry bread crumbs
Even the clouds are loath to appear
On this stifling summer afternoon
Alone sits the lotus
Spreading the tranquility
Ripples ring outward over the water
The lily pads tremble
Startling drowsy crows in the trees
Splash! A frog jumps in the pond

芒種

梅子已黃，雨兀自飄落
泥濘的巷中，有人
披著被遺棄多年的簑衣
匆匆俯首而過，斑駁的
土墙，挽留不住他的腳步
一九七九年初夏，在南台灣
小港的山裡，我見過
這樣一幅難以忘懷的畫面
水漬努力地攀住頹墙
隨即又癱軟墜下

簑衣、竹笠以及農具
至今依舊令人喜愛，逗留在
精緻彩印的畫刊裡
一九八六年春末，在大台北
舊書肆的角落，我發現
來自香港的曆書攤著
線裝、霉爛、粗黑的宋體字
羞怯地解釋安床與納畜
店外呼嘯而過刺耳的車聲
黃燈閃爍，雨兀自飄落

Grain in Ear

The plums have turned a ripe yellow, a drifting rain falls
In a muddy lane, a man in a straw
Rain cape of the kind not seen for years
Hurriedly walks past the mottled
Earthen wall without pausing
Early summer, 1979, in southern Taiwan
On a hill in Xiaogang I saw this
Unforgettable scene:
The rain beat down and seemed to climb the wall
Then fall back again

Straw rain capes, bamboo hats, and farm tools
Still loved by the people, appear
In slick pictorials
At the end of spring, 1986, I found
A mildewed, thread-bound almanac from Hong Kong
In the corner of a used bookstore
Its big Song-style characters
Humbly gave auspicious days for moving and buying livestock
Outside the shop honking cars passed
Yellow lamplight shimmered in the drifting rain

夏至

跟著夏天，我們行經
翠綠的山谷，三色堇沿途
歡呼，漫生的孟宗掃開了
一條窄仄的路，偶而竄出
灰白的影子，呵你看松鼠
　　（秋天還遠──是誰多事
　　趕著夏天剪落了松子）
倏忽爬上松林，瞪著眼珠
跟著我們，這樹跳過那樹
夏天，尾隨松鼠而至

尾隨松鼠，我們也踏入
鼠尾草四散的小徑，淡紫色
鋸齒葉，帶些未被賞識的幽怨
　　（夏天真到了嗎？蜂蝶
　　還癡心戀著杜鵑）
每隔幾步，給我們一個回眸
啊你看八色鳥，踩著碎步
正在林下嘰喳啄食
我們跟著夏天走進山谷
夏天，跟著八色鳥而至

Summer Solstice

In summer we walk through
A green valley, tricolor violets along the way
Shout for joy, the thick dwarf bamboo sweeps over
The narrow road, occasionally a squirrel darts
From the shadows, see it . . .
    (Autumn is a long way off—who is busy
    gathering pinecones in summer?)
Scamper up the pine tree, watching us
It follows, leaping from tree to tree
Summer arrives on the tail of a squirrel

On the tail of a squirrel we enter
A small path edged with purple sage
Serrated leaves bear the sorrow of being unappreciated
    (Is summer really here? Bees and butterflies
    are still infatuated with the azaleas)
Every few steps it looks back at us
Look! A pheasant moves with short, quick steps
Clucks, pecking for food under the trees
With summer we enter a valley
Summer arrives with a pheasant

小暑

推開窗子，首先是烏雲
把錯落著的大廈逐一捏住
眼下是棋盤一樣的街和路
瘦瘦小小，疾行的車
一下子啟動一下子煞住
再遠些，是河流銜著橋
再遠些，是橋扯著山麓
再遠些，是山麓扛著雲
再遠些，就一切都不見了
只有靜止的風醞釀著陣雨

關上窗子，背後也是世界
卷宗錯落，壓住辦公桌
椅子畏縮，退了兩三步
萬年青青在牆角
一半兒嫩綠一半兒黃熟
再近些，是殘稿纏著字紙簍
再近些，是字紙簍陪著風扇
再近些，風扇掀開了計劃書
再近些，電話急急跳起腳來
唾沫橫飛在話筒的另一頭

Lesser Heat

Opening the window, I see black clouds
Catch the disorderly skyscrapers one by one
Below, the streets are laid out like a chessboard
Small and slender, the fast cars
Stop and start
Farther off, the river grips the bridge
Still farther, the bridge pulls the foot of the mountains
Still farther, the mountains shoulder the clouds
Still farther, nothing can be seen
Except rain brewing in the still air

Closing the window, a world exists behind me
Files piled in disorder on the desk
The chair pushed back two or three steps
Evergreen in the corner
Pale green and dingy yellow
A little closer, crumpled papers in a wastepaper basket
Still closer, the wastepaper basket accompanied by a fan
Still closer, the fan opens a calendar
Still closer, the telephone jumps
Spraying speech from the other end

大暑

熱，從冷中來　　　冷向熱中去
整座城市喧鬧著　　在漸寒的夜裏
在孤寂的燈下　　　思念如火
愛情被草草埋葬　　痛，走入心肺
被拋置於誓辭上　　都已冰涼了
窗口的滿天星　　　滿天的星
燦然怒放著　　　　呼喚著
那年夏天的歎息　　你的名字與形影
熱辣辣劃過　　　　從我眼前
鬱悶的風中　　　　一顆星子滑落

一顆星子滑落　　　鬱悶的風中
從我眼前　　　　　熱辣辣劃過
你的名字與形影　　那年夏天的歎息
呼喚著　　　　　　燦然怒放著
滿天的星　　　　　窗口的滿天星
都已冰涼了　　　　被拋置於誓辭上
痛，走入心肺　　　愛情被草草埋葬
思念如火　　　　　在孤寂的燈下
在漸寒的夜裏　　　整座城市喧鬧著
冷向熱中去　　　　熱，從冷中來

Great Heat

Heat out of cold
The city clamors
Under a solitary lamp
Love buried carelessly
Discarded for an oath
Skyful of stars in the window
Glowing fully
The sighs that summer
Pass hotly
In a stifling wind

Cold into heat
On a slowly cooling night
Longing like fire
Pain enters the heart
Freezes
Sky full of stars
Called out
Your name and figure
Before my eyes
A star falls

A star falls
Before my eyes
Your name and figure
Called out
Sky full of stars
Freezes
Pain enters the heart
Longing like fire
On a slowly cooling night
Cold into heat

In a stifling wind
Pass hotly
The sighs that summer
Glowing fully
Skyful of stars in the window
Discarded for an oath
Love buried carelessly
Under a solitary lamp
The city clamors
Heat out of cold

立秋

愛情像槭樹的葉子
慢慢褪色。親愛的
理想多半也是這樣
像平原上的列車
在黯夜中一節節遁走
遁走的，其聲隆隆
褪去的，已難補救
親愛的，別擔心
褪去的是青澀
將來就是紅熟

歲月殘憾猶如綠葉
落水漂走。親愛的
生命有時也會如此
像山崖上的滾石
在風雨前一顆顆跌落
跌落的，其聲空空
漂走的，無法捕捉
親愛的，別難過
漂走了暑夏
換來了涼秋

Beginning of Autumn

Love is like the maple leaf
That slowly fades. Beloved,
Ideals are much the same
Like a train on the flat lands
Fleeing in the dark of night
Fleeing, rattling on
Once gone, they won't come back
Beloved, don't worry
Astringent green gives way
To ripe red

Time is imperfect as a green leaf
That falls in the water and drifts away.
Beloved, the same too can be said of life
Like stones falling from a precipice
Falling one after another before a storm
Falling, their empty sounds
Drift away, they cannot be held back
Beloved, don't be sad
The great heat drifts away
Giving way to cool autumn

處暑

潛伏在最黑最黯處的
是還戀愛著光的暑氣
夜色已一舉謀殺了夕陽
幽靈還在空蕩的原野上
空蕩地飄，幽靈還在
空蕩的河川中空蕩地
漂。空蕩地飄著
竹燈籠。空蕩地漂著
小水燈。空蕩地飄呀漂著
暗戀著光明的黑夜

給竹籠燈，夜才有溫暖
給水燈燭，黑才有依靠
給流離以安慰，土地就不愁煞
給冤曲以平反，天空就不肅殺
給孤魂給野鬼以三牲水果
生與死就不致大動干戈
給最黑給最黯，以微光以微熱
陰沈的風將會破涕歡樂
給乾渴的井以水聲
愛，澆息了恨火

The Limit of Heat

Concealed in the darkest place
Is the light-loving heat of summer
Night has murdered the setting sun
There are still spirits on the empty plain
Floating emptily, there are still spirits
In the empty rivers, floating
Emptily. Floating emptily
In a lantern set adrift. Floating emptily
A lamp. Secretly in love
With the light, the night floats emptily

A lamp gives warmth to the night
A floating lamp supports the night
By giving comfort to a wanderer,
the land is sad no more
By giving justice to the wronged, the sky is grave no more
By giving offerings of meat and fruit to the ghosts and lonely spirits
The dead and living cease to war
By giving light and warmth to the darkness
The gloomy wind sings with joy
By giving the sound of water to a dry well
Love extinguishes the fire of hate

白露

一滴露珠閃閃發亮
在晨曦前鷹架的鋼柱上
微微傾墜，把漸藍的天
斜斜踩到對街高樓
刀刃一般切割出的牆緣
水泥散置，在工地
守夜的人仍打盹
在挖土機的履帶前
整座城市還沒醒來
一個呵欠，從夏天打到秋天

一個小孩，從後面盪到前面
在工地後側公園內
跟秋天一起盪鞦韆
他前仰他後俯他睜眼他閉眼
地球跟著陶醉了
一棟大廈挨著一棟大廈
頂住即將傾斜的天
露珠一樣，一路蔓延
都市也跟著小孩
露珠一樣盪過天邊

White Dew

Just before dawn a drop of dew shines
On the iron construction scaffolding
Hanging at a slight angle, it reflects the slowly bluing sky
It leans toward the building across the street
Which like a knife shaves off the edge of the wall
Concrete is scattered around the construction site
The night watchman is still napping
In front of the backhoe
The city sleeps
One long yawn from summer to autumn

A child swings
In the park behind the construction site
He swings with autumn
Swinging back and forth, eyes closed, eyes opened
The world is drunk too
The high-rises lean against each other
To hold up the falling sky
Like a rolling drop of dew
The city follows the boy
Who, like the dewdrop, swings at the edge of the sky

秋分

給我一塊土地
黃澄的稻穗
掃出晴藍的天
鮮紅的楓葉
喚醒翠綠的山
給我一塊土地
清水漾盪在河中
白雲徘徊到窗前
給我這個夢
夢中的夢想昨天已被實現

給我一塊土地
黑濁的癈水
養肥腥臭的魚
灰茫的毒氣
充實迷路的雲
給我一塊土地
稻穗蛻變成煙囪
森林精簡為廠棚
給我這個夢
夢中的夢想明天將會完成

Autumn Equinox

Give me a piece of land
Where yellow rice plants
Sweep the blue sky
Where bright red maple leaves
Waken the green hills
Give me a piece of land
Where clear water ripples in the rivers
Where white clouds linger before my window
Give me such a dream
Perhaps the dream in a dream came true yesterday

Give me a piece of land
With black, dirty water
For raising fat, smelly fish
Where the gray, poisonous air
Is stocked with stray clouds
Give me a piece of land
Where the rice plants have become chimneys
And the forests have turned into factories
Give me such a dream
Where the dream in a dream will come true tomorrow

寒露

雨從昨夜起
就一路下個不停
通過鬱黑的甬道
通過無夢的黎明
在最先醒來的煞車聲中
暫停。縱向車道紅燈
橫向綠燈，川流湧動
是熱滾滾的人群
冷漠洗在臉上
洗掉了青春

水花激切，腳步急促
只有廣告牌定定站著
把媚眼拋給旋飛的鴿群
簽到簿打卡鐘積秒成分
這些交錯的顏面未知的姓名
都會被收進檔案保存
留下一些徬徨的腳步
噓寒噓給自己聽
他們有緣邂逅水露
熱情卻被凍成冰冷

Cold Dew

The rain began last night
It has rained without stopping
Through the dark wet passageway
Through dreamless dawn
It stops momentarily
As the first braking cars are heard
For one direction, a red light
For the other, a green light, a surging current, a warm,
      bustling crowd
Faces bathed in coldness
Youth washed away

The foam too candid, the footsteps too hasty
Only the billboard is motionless
Fluttering its lashes at the pigeons
Minutes adding up on the time clock
These nameless. changing faces
Will soon be filed away
A few hesitant steps left behind
Greeting one another
They meet by chance of fate
But their warmth has been frozen

霜降

霜，降自北，一路鋪向南方
沿黑亮的鐵軌，幻影
飄過城市、窮鄉與僻壤
在平交道前兜了一圈
回來偎著小站店家的看板
偶而閃過夜行的車燈
一兩聲燒肉粽的叫喊
還有ラジオ中的補破網
八〇年代末葉的台灣
傳唱四〇年代初期的音響

鄉愁通常也是這樣，北上
在卡拉OK頭前叫爸叫母
酒罐爛醉，橫七八豎在桌腳
白沫沸騰，霜一樣降在桌上
所謂文化是東洋換西洋
所謂古蹟是被推倒的城牆
民俗躍上花車——所謂觀光
是姑娘的大腿大家同齊來觀賞
中產階級們暢論世界與前瞻
霜降，在他們憂國憂民的髮上

Hoar Frost

The frost spreads from north to south
Along the shinning black rails, an illusion
It drifts over cities, poor and remote places
Circles a railroad crossing
Then nestles on a shop sign at a little railway station,
Illumined by cars passing in the night
Snatches of "Buy My Dumplings" are heard
"Mending Broken Nets" is on the radio
Taiwan at the end of the eighties
Playing and singing songs from the early forties.

That's the way homesickness is, up north
Crying for mom and pop in a Karaoke bar
Beer cans and wine bottles lie scattered under the tables
Heads of white foam rise and fall like frost on the table
So-called culture is the western replacing the eastern
Historic sites are demolished walls
Folk customs ride a flowery float, and sight-seeing
Is a young woman's thigh that everyone enjoys together
The middle class discusses the world and the future
Frost falls on the hair of those concerned for the world

立冬

隨寒風入山，棧道危橋
一路奔逐青苔咬住的地表
飛霧從另一座山的身後
迅即掩住，踩涓細的
水聲，叫醒了冬
又迅即離去。留下
松樹幾株，依舊堅持
不為季候風所動的綠
以及陽光，敲叩著台灣杉
像啄木鳥敲叩著清晨一樣

像啄木鳥敲叩著清晨，一樣
陽光敲叩在中央山脈的背上
放眼左右，望北向南
百餘座山頭爭相探入
海拔三千公尺以上的高空
危哉險矣！北風也因而驚懼
岩岸之後是大洋
砂岸之前是海峽
冬，畏畏縮縮在雲中
忍不住叫出：*Ilhas Formosas*

Beginning of Winter

It follows the cold wind into the mountains,
Racing over precipitous roads and dangerous bridges
Over the moss-eaten terrain
Mist flies over the mountains
Covering all, trampling the faint sound
Of flowing water, waking winter
And passing on just as quickly. It leaves behind
Evergreen pines
Which do not yield to the monsoons
And sunlight taps on the Taiwan firs
The way a woodpecker knocks on morning

A woodpecker knocks on morning
The way sunlight taps on the central range
Looking left and right, north and south
A hundred peaks strive to penetrate the sky
Three thousand meters above sea level
How magnificent! Even the north wind is stunned
Beyond the rocky coast is the Pacific
Before the sandy coast is the Strait
Winter recoils in the clouds
And shouts: *Ilhas Formosas*

小雪

小雪趕在紅葉之後
開遍愛荷華初冬的山坡
彷彿落葉一般，不斷飛過
我暫時寄寓的樓窗前
又頹然歇下腳來
在輕迴的風中，在自己
也決定不了的處所
呵了一口氣，灰濛濛的
天空——另一半正注視著
大洋彼端的家國

思念有時像小雪。有時
更像落葉，不融不化
只是慢慢腐萎
這異國晨間的細雪
疑是昨夜的一場夢魘
夢中，已經死去的父親
也來與我站在窗前
指著四處飄零的雪花
說：雪太冷了，我們回去
回到故鄉舖滿落葉的土地

Lesser Snow

After the red leaves have dropped, a light snow falls
Covering the Iowa hillsides in early winter
Like falling leaves, it drifts without letting up
Past the window of my temporary abode
It pauses to rest
In the swift wind, in a place
Not of my choosing, I
Heave a sigh as the other half of the ashen
Sky watches
My home on the other side of the sea

Sometimes longing is like a light snow. Sometimes
It's more like the falling leaves that don't melt
But just slowly rot away
The fine snow on a morning in this foreign land
Can it be the bad dream of last night?
In which my late father
Came and stood before my window
And pointing to the snow falling all around
He said: "The snow is too cold, let's go
Home where the fallen leaves carpet the ground."

大雪

一棵小樹在雪中
流淚。一棟屋子
在雪中流盪。一
扇窗子在雪中流
散。一把椅子在
雪中流離。一片
田野在雪中流浪
。一道河川在雪
中流失。一個人
在雪中，流血。

雪在一棵小樹旁
流淚。雪在一棟
屋子前流盪。雪
在一扇窗子前流
散。雪在一把椅
子下流離。雪在
一片田野裡流浪
。雪在一道河川
內流失。雪在一
個人心上流血。

Great Snow

A small tree cries
In the snow. A house drifts
In the snow. A window vanishes
In the snow. A chair sits destitute
In the snow. A field wanders
In the snow. A river disappears
In the snow. A person bleeds
In the snow.

The snow cries beside
A tree. The snow drifts around
A house. The snow vanishes before
A window. The snow lies destitute under
A chair. The snow wanders in
A field. The snow disappears in
A river. The snow bleeds in
A person's heart.

冬至

仍然記得兒時，記得
兒時被鞭炮聲喚起來的夜
輕煙輕輕，撲著我們
滾熱的是圓仔湯
冽寒的是路上霜
松果一般，我們跑過
山坡、草坪、家門口
天色有時藍有時灰
枯枝招手在山頭
圈圈年輪圈下了歡樂

如今我們走入燈火，走入
燈火喧嘩、躍動的市街
輕煙輕輕，追著我們
微弱的是鼻息
強勁的是煙塵
瓶蓋一樣，我們墜落
酒廊、舞廳、三溫暖
方向有時左有時右
酒矸搖頭在街頭
急急煞車急死了憂愁

Winter Solstice

I still remember when I was a child, I remember
The night I was awakened by firecrackers
How the smoke assailed us
The rice ball soup was boiling hot
The frost on the road was freezing cold
Like pinecones, we roved
The slopes, the meadows, and in front of the house
Sometimes the sky was blue, sometimes grey
Withered branches waved from the mountains
Joy circled on the annual rings of trees

Today we step into the lights
The clamoring lights and the bustling streets
The smoke follows us
Our breathing labored
The pollution strong
Like bottle caps we fall in
Bars, dance halls, and bathhouses
Sometimes left, sometimes right
On the street, a drunk shakes his head
Melancholy is killed by squealing brakes

小寒

一隻小鳥向天空求救
一隻小鳥向大地求救
天空很大方
垂下厚重的烏雲歡迎牠
大地很慷慨
舖上銀亮的冰雪保護牠
這隻小鳥雙翅瑟縮
這隻小鳥渾身戰抖
求救，求救
天地含笑聽牠的啁啾

一隻小鳥要救天空
一隻小鳥要救大地
天空不開口
開出羅網網羅牠
大地不設防
設下囚牢牢囚牠
這隻小鳥控訴天空
這隻小鳥控訴大地
掉光了翅膀換成雪花
雪花飄飄，埋葬了牠

Lesser Cold

A small bird asks the sky for help
A small bird asks the land for help
The sky is generous
Hanging thick, dark clouds in welcome
The land is generous
Laying a carpet of bright, silver snow for shelter
The small bird's wings tremble
The small bird's body shakes
Help, help
The sky and the land smile hearing its cries

A small bird wants to help the sky
A small bird wants to help the land
The sky is silent
It casts a net to catch the bird
The land is defenseless
It builds a prison to hold the bird captive
The small bird accuses the sky
The small bird accuses the land
Its feathers fall, turned to snowflakes
It's buried by drifting snowflakes

大寒

這時候，他們都該已就寢了
床頭燈緩緩地熄滅了
窗帘也靜靜地闔攏了
街道沉默在街樹的沉默中
橋墩隱蔽在橋樑的隱蔽下
這時候他們，都該已睡著了
島嶼蜷曲在海洋的被褥裡
大陸袒身於沙漠的枕頭邊
亞洲跟美洲擠在一塊取暖
南極和北極互相使著眼色

這時候他們都該已，入夢了
地球急急從軌道拋離
星雲疾疾自大氣現出
有些粒子繼續反目
有些物質開始燕好
這時候，他們，都該已，睡熟了
被放捨的我仰望夜空
在巨蛇一般蜿蜒的星海中
再也找不到他們入夢的太陽系
再也找不到他們就寢的地球

Great Cold

By this time they should all be asleep
The lamp on the nightstand slowly goes out
The drawn curtains hang motionless
The streets are silent among the silent trees
The bridge pier is hidden beneath the spans
By this time they should all be asleep
The island curls up in a bedding of sea
The mainland lies uncovered on a desert pillow
Together Asia and America seek warmth
The North and South Poles exchange looks

By this time they should all be dreaming
The Earth quickly leaves its rails
Nebulae appear in space
Particles continue to war
Substances begin to merge
By this time they should all be asleep
Abandoned, I look up at the night sky
In a sea of stars that slithers like a giant snake
I cannot find the solar system of their dreams
Nor can I see the earth where they sleep

XIANG YANG (Hsiang Yang) is the penname of Lin Qiyang. He was born in Nantou, Taiwan in 1955. As an undergraduate he studied Japanese and subsequently received an MA in journalism from the Culture University and a PhD in journalism from National Chengchi University. He participated in the University of Iowa International Writing Program. Over the years, he has worked as a newspaper editor and has taught at a number of universities in Taiwan. In addition to being a prominent poet, he is a well-known essayist and has also written scholarly and critical works as well as books for children. He is also a woodblock print artist. These days he is actively engaged in using social media for promoting cultural and historical activities.

JOHN BALCOM holds a PhD in Chinese and Comparative Literature from Washington University in St Louis. An award winning translator of Chinese literature, philosophy, and children's books, he teaches translation at the Monterey Institute of International Studies, where he ran the Chinese program for many years. His translations include *Taiwan's Indigenous Writers: An Anthology of Stories, Essays, and Poems*, *After Many Autumns: An Anthology of Chinese Buddhist Literature*, *There's Nothing I Can Do When I Think of you Late at Night* by Cao Naiqian, and *Trees without Wind* by Li Rui. He is a past president of the American Literary Translators Association.

Also Available from Zephyr Press by John Balcom:
(ISBN 978-0-939010-83-7) Lo Fu *Driftwood*
(ISBN 978-0-981552-11-8) Lo Fu *Stone Cell*